IBRAIM ROCHA

UNVEILING PLATO AND ARISOTLE IN DWORKIN'S THOUGHT

IBRAIM ROCHA

UNVEILING PLATO AND ARISOTLE IN DWORKIN'S THOUGHT

Elements for the interpretation of Fundamental Rights

ScienciaScripts

Imprint

Any brand names and product names mentioned in this book are subject to trademark, brand or patent protection and are trademarks or registered trademarks of their respective holders. The use of brand names, product names, common names, trade names, product descriptions etc. even without a particular marking in this work is in no way to be construed to mean that such names may be regarded as unrestricted in respect of trademark and brand protection legislation and could thus be used by anyone.

Cover image: www.ingimage.com

This book is a translation from the original published under ISBN 978-3-330-19658-2.

Publisher:
Sciencia Scripts
is a trademark of
Dodo Books Indian Ocean Ltd., member of the OmniScriptum S.R.L Publishing group
str. A.Russo 15, of. 61, Chisinau-2068, Republic of Moldova Europe
Printed at: see last page
ISBN: 978-620-4-08494-7

IBRAIM ROCHA

Doctor in Human Rights and Environment/UFPA; Master in Civil Procedural Law/UFPA, Lawyer in the Environmental and Agrarian areas (Rocha e Menezes Law Firm), State Attorney of the State of Pará, Former State Attorney General of the State of Pará (2007-2010), Former author of several legal articles, monographs and collective works in the legal area, with emphasis on Public Civil Action and Labor Procedure (Ltr); Co-partnership, Effects of the Judgment and Judgment on Collective Redress (Forense), Constitutional Agrarian Law: Lessons in Agri-Environmental Law (Forum)

SUMMARY

The purpose of this booklet is to present a reading that reveals the points of connection between Ronald Dworkin's work and the work of Plato and Aristotle, allowing a better reading of Dworkin as a path to the effectiveness of Fundamental Rights, through a more consistent interpretive practice through the exercise of integrity.

CONTENT

1. Introduction

Awakened to the purpose of philosophy, Benedito Nunes, when inquiring about the advent of the *overcoming of philosophy,* places the diversity of the products of human culture as manifestations of the Spirit's journey that takes place in it, therefore, the return to philosophy is what will allow us to reach the bosom of the absolute, of human plenitude, and that synthesizes as follows:

> Thus, denying itself first as exteriority in Nature, and then denying itself as isolated consciousness - in order to universalize itself in the objective forms of Morals, Law and State -, exteriorizing itself afterwards in Art - in order to, afterwards, interiorize itself in the religious feeling -, the Spirit only in philosophy, the last scale of its process, will reach the full consciousness of itself, when, then, it knows everything as its own form and recognizes itself in each one of its forms. It is in this relationship of knowledge and recognition that the Spirit embraces the whole reality, dialectically explained or totalized, and reverted to the bosom of the absolute[1]

The purpose of this text, following these footsteps, is to reveal Dworkin's connections with Plato and also with Aristotle, finding the path that unites them, which facilitates and improves the reading of Dworkin's work, with gains for the practice and understanding of Law.

This allows us to recognize Law as a form of philosophizing, whose interpretative practice serves as an instrument for the effectiveness of the protection of fundamental rights.

---

[1]NUNES, Benedito. *The overcoming of Philosophy* In O Dorso do Tigre. São Paulo: Ed 34, 2009. p.

2. Overcoming the Curse of TOT

Plato, in *Fedro,* relates the myth that there was in the vicinity of Náucratis, in Egypt, an old divinity who was known by the name of Tot, and who was the first to discover numbers and calculation, geometry and astronomy, the game of backgammon and dice, and also the characters of writing. At this time Tamus reigned over all Egypt, and was sought out by Tot, who presented his arts to him, with the suggestion that they be taught to the Egyptians. The king then asked what they were all for, and as Tot explained them, he either criticized or praised them. King Tamus made remarks for and against each of the arts. However, when he came to the characters of writing, Tot said that it presented a discipline capable of making the Egyptians wiser and with better memory, discovering the remedy for forgetfulness and ignorance. When he finished speaking the King assured him:

> Ingenious as you are, Tot, it is one thing to invent the arts, and quite another to discourse on their utility or disadvantage to those who have to make use of them. Such is the case with you, as the father of writing: because of the affection you attach to it, you attribute to it exactly the opposite action to that which is proper to it, for it is quite suitable to bring forgetfulness to the soul of the one who learns, because it does not oblige him to exercise his memory. Those who trust to writing will be by external means, with the aid of strange characters, not in their own inmost being, and thanks to themselves, that they will awaken their reminiscences. You have not discovered the remedy for memory, but only for remembrance. What you offer to those who study is mere appearance of knowledge, not reality itself. After hearing a world of things, without having learned anything, they will consider themselves ultra-wise, when, for the most part, they are only ignorant, pseudo-wise, simply not really wise. (PLATO, *Fedro*, 274 E - 275 B) [2]

[2]PLATO. *Fedro*. Greek text John Burnet. Translation Carlos Alberto Nunes. 3. ed. Belém: Edufpa, 2011b. p. 183.

For Law to fulfill its role it must move away the *curse of Tot* from the interpretation of fundamental rights, building its substantial content beyond the reading of the constitutional text, highlighting the role of the interpreter to reveal the written text, which without it says nothing, which is mute and no other way finds to express the purposes and values of the community.

This is all the more appropriate in an era when people think that the millions of computerised files available on the Internet reveal the great wisdom of society, when it may reveal exactly the opposite, when we fail to investigate what moral and political values this information is at the service of. Therefore, legal interpretation, as a characteristic element of the Integrity of Law, cannot consider the existence of the written text sufficient to reveal the best purpose of the community.

The myth of Tot makes it clear that one cannot be fascinated by language and take words as if they were living objects with a will of their own. It warns that even written knowledge necessarily needs the human being who interprets it in order to effectively have any meaning, and that written knowledge alone is of no use. See Socrates' argument in *Fedro:*

> The fact is, Philo, that writing is very dangerous, and in this respect it is very like painting, for the latter presents its products as living, but if anyone asks it a question, it remains silent with dignity. It is the same with writing. You are inclined to think that you are conversing with intelligent beings; but if, with your desire to learn, you question them about what they say, they only answer in one way and always the same thing. Once they have definitively fixed their writing, they roll on from here to there, without the slightest discourse, both among those who know the subject and those who have nothing to do with it, without knowing to whom they should address themselves and to whom they should not. And in case they are unjustly attacked or belittled, they will never dispense with paternal help, because by themselves they are as incapable of defending themselves as of helping anyone. [3]

---

[3]PLATO. *Fedro*. Greek text John Burnet. Translation Carlos Alberto Nunes. 3. ed. Belém: Edufpa, 2011b. p. 185.

Although there is always doubt of one's own certainties, this allows one to act as a sower, who, faced with the uncertainty of harvesting the best fruit, seeks to cultivate the best soil to plant the best seed, so that the best result may bear fruit (PLATO, *Fedro*, 276 B)[4]. So we can see that the myth of Tot is present in Dworkin's thought, when he states that the Law is an interpretive practice, and without which it is not possible to understand what the Law is.

---

[4]"LXII. SOCRATES: That's the one. And now, tell me this: would an intelligent farmer who took an interest in his seeds and was determined to see them bear fruit, go and sow them, in the middle of summer, in some garden of Adonis, to rejoice at the beautiful spectacle of germination in eight days? If he would do so, it would be for amusement and on the occasion of some festival, would he not? But the seeds that were truly dear to him, he would entrust to the appropriate soil, according to the rules of agriculture, considering himself very happy if eight months later all of them had germinated with perfection" PLATO. *Philo*. Greek text John Burnet. Translation Carlos Alberto Nunes. 3. ed. Belém: Edufpa, 2011b. p. 187.

3. Philosophical Attitude and Constructive Interpretation - Identity of Goals

Since the beginning of modern philosophy, despite diverging on the path, Plato and Aristotle created methods, through which they sought answers to the fundamental questions of humanity, and, although they disagreed on the form of asking, it is possible to identify in these authors the common link of recognizing that only the human being, by being able to formulate principles, could find the truth, even if by divergence of method. One sought the reality of *being* as a reflection of ideas; the other intended to reach them based on *being*.

Thus, Plato and Aristotle, as true philosophers, did not sustain skepticism about the possibility of humanity reaching the truth, they could diverge as to the method, but they were firm in their purpose of, through correctly formulated questions, obtaining answers founded on principles and therefore true.

In book I, chapter VII, of the Metaphysics, after, in the antecedents, having carried out a rescue of the theories about the origin of being since the pre-Socratics and announcing the criticism of Plato's theory of ideas, Aristotle presents the assertion that, although no one has reached quidity and substance with clarity, recognizes that "nearer to it approach those who admit the ideas"[5] and concludes by acknowledging that only by principles is it possible to reach the truth stating that "evidently the principles must be studied, either all like this, or in any of these ways"[6].

This recognition is fundamental because it reveals the unity of Platonic and Aristotelian thought about the possibility of successful access to knowledge

---

[5] ARISTOTELES. *Metaphysics*. Translation Vinzenzo Cocco and notes by Joaquim de Carvalho. São Paulo: Abril Cutural, 1979. Book II. p. 26. (Collection the Thinkers).
[6] ARISTOTELES. *Metaphysics*. Translation Vinzenzo Cocco and notes by Joaquim de Carvalho. São Paulo: Abril Cutural, 1979. Book II. p. 26. (Collection the Thinkers).

by human reason through the formulation of principles, even if divergent on the method to be followed for this purpose, which is the permanent task of the whole of humanity, well synthesized by Aristotle in Chapter I of Book II of the Metaphysics:

> Speculation about truth is in one sense difficult, in another easy; the proof is that no one can completely attain it, nor completely depart from it, and that every philosopher has something to say about nature, each one adding nothing or little to the truth, although one makes of the whole of all a good harvest(Metaphysica, Book II, Chap. I, 1). [7]

Exactly because of the greatness of their thoughts, until today the same question is often returned, in which the method is confused with the objective, and they are clearly divergent as to how to walk. This distinction does not seem fundamental, since these greatest thinkers of humanity had already recognized that the essential is the construction of principles as a result of the use of reason in the understanding of the object, independent of the type of object studied, which evidently forces changes in the method of approach. Thus, aware of this trap that logical reasoning can lead to, Aristotle had already warned that: "That is why it is important to know how each thing is to be accepted, for it is absurd to seek at the same time science and the method of science: neither of them, for it is easy to learn" (Metaphysics, Book II, chapter II, 4) [8]

The lesson that can be drawn is that in spite of severe limitations, the whole of human thought can, step by step, overcome the limits of knowledge, however, the essential thing for obtaining the knowledge of truth is not to test the method, but the principle obtained by reason. Thus, if the principle is placed as truth from the method, it can be stated that this constitutes a serious error for the

---

[7]ARISTOTELES. *Metaphysics*. Translation Vinzenzo Cocco and notes by Joaquim de Carvalho. São Paulo: Abril Cultural, 1979. Book II. p. 39. (Collection the Thinkers).
[8]ARISTOTELES. *Metaphysics*. Translation Vinzenzo Cocco and notes by Joaquim de Carvalho. São Paulo: Abril Cultural, 1979. Book II. p. 43. (Collection the Thinkers)

correction of thought. In this way, there is no superior proof of a principle or of a science by reason of the method it uses. A principle can be tested for its correctness only at the level of argumentation, because the fundamental is not the path, but the objective of the path, that is, the formation of true judgments by means of principles[9].

Dwokin adopts this path of principles and, even without stating it, it is possible to find elements of a fundamental rights theory in his work, when it is observed that the interpretative criteria he uses aim at the construction of the value Justice from constitutional principles. His work is a large set of arguments on the substance of what the best principles should guide the community.

This form of reasoning is fundamentally Platonic and Aristotelian. And because they are principles they may be object of disagreement among the recipients of their application, and such disagreement can only be resolved through their interpretation, so the search for the right answer is nothing more than the normal path of this classical method of philosophizing. Ronald Dworkin, although not affirming a concept of principles, consistent with his criticism to the semantic theories of law, teaches that the rule of law can only be achieved from

---

[9] In the booklet *The Idea of Good between Plato and Aristotle,* Hans-Georg Gadamer makes an interesting philosophical exercise of constructing a dialogue between the principles of Platonic and Aristotelian philosophy, although underlining their distinction, but emphasizing that in the field of practical philosophy (moral) there is an evident convergence between these thinkers, as he details especially in chapter V of the book, and, for this very reason, right in the *Presentation of the Problem,* he stresses that "Hodiernally, it should be taken for granted that we, in the whole of Aristotle's legacy, have not returned, nowhere, to a point where Aristotle has ceased to criticise Plato's theory of ideas, in the same way that we have not arrived at a point where he has also ceased to be a Platonic". Cf. GADAMER, Hans-Georg. The *idea of the good between Plato and Aristotle.* Translation Tito Lívio Cruz Romano. São Paulo: Martins Fontes, 2009, p. 10. An example of this assertion can be found in the Aristotelian text *On the Soul,* in which although Aristotle criticizes those who, like Plato, "They only strive, however, to say what kind of thing the soul is; about the body which houses it, they define nothing else, as if it were possible, according to the Pythagorean myths, for a soul at random to lodge in any body" (407b, 20) he does not fail to conclude like Plato that there is an indivisible nature of the soul which even allows for the unity of the body, even though for him the soul cannot be explained without the body, so he questions and answers: "Then what unifies the soul, if it is indivisible by nature? It is certainly not the body: rather it seems, on the contrary, that the soul unifies the body; at least, the body dissipates and destroys itself with the departure of the soul" (411b, 5). ARISTOTHES. *On the soul.* Translation Ana Maria Lóio. São Paulo: Martins Fontes, 2013. p. 33-34.

the interpretation of the Constitution[10]. The constitutional rules that establish fundamental rights and their effectiveness cannot do without their interpretation, because the fact that they are founded only on principles does not deny nor is it a sufficient reason to affirm the lack of effectiveness or cogency of fundamental rights; on the contrary, it is through the interpretation of principles that fundamental rights are better and effectively realized in the world of law.

But this does not mean that for Dworkin the interpretive theory should be linked to the interpretation of fundamental rights based only on the law as it stands, because the interpretation of the principles cannot be limited to the letter of the law, but should consider elements of history, morality and ethics, from which the legal system originates, without which it is not possible to perform the legal interpretation, giving the exact contours of the law. As the text of the Constitution does not solve the difficult cases, it is necessary that its interpreters look for something other than the words so that they can perform their work, Ronald Dworkin does not present a concept of the nature of constitutional principles, but this can be built from his concept of law as interpretation, from the practice of the Judiciary, in which he highlights the judicial argumentative procedure, not because it is only important, but because he recognizes the central role that this argumentative form plays within legal

---

[10]It is important to note that for Dworkin "Law as integrity condemns activism and any practice of constitutional jurisdiction that is close to it. It insists that judges apply the Constitution through interpretation, not by *fiat,* meaning that their decisions must adjust to constitutional practice, not ignore it. DWORKIN, Ronald. *The Empire of Law.* São Paulo: Martins Fontes, 1999. p. 452. In original "Law as integrity condemns activism, and any practicy of constitutional adjucations close to it. It insists that justices inforce the Constitution through interpretation, not fiat, meaning that decisions must fit constitutional practice, not ignore it" DWORKIN, Ronald. *Law's empire.* Cambridge: Harvard University Press, 1986. p. 378. As Atienza points out, in the current democratic societies it is fundamental to explain Law from its understanding as argumentation, because it is essential to observe that ~~the~~ forms of interpretation may even lead to reveal our conception of democracy, by which it is required that legal decisions are understandable and acceptable by citizens, for this reason he considers that it is fundamental to state that law is not only concerned with formal values (predictability of decisions, legal security), but also with material values such as truth and justice, and political values of consensus acceptance. Cf. ATIENZA, Manuel. *El sentido del derecho.* Barcelona: Ariel, 2004. p. 263-264.

practice, because they are more explicit and have an influence on other forms of legal discourse without the same reciprocity[11].

Dworkin rejects the literal interpretation as a method of understanding the law and other similar forms that he calls semantic theories of law, whose most important form is positivism, because the law cannot be a simple matter of fact, or just an empirical issue, rather than a theoretical one. The exact understanding of the law requires interpretative attitude that is not conversional, because in this one, we only try to understand what the author intends to tell us, but it requires a *constructive* interpretative attitude, according to the model of creative interpretation, related to the arts and social practices, in which the purpose is highlighted more than the cause, mirroring the purpose of the interpreter that the object or practice analyzed is seen as the best possible example of the genre to which it belongs [12].

Aristotle had already exposed the idea that to argue constructively it is necessary to establish premises of the purpose that is intended to obtain with the argument. Thus, he states that "We must distinguish as many meanings as serve our purpose. For example, if we wish to argue constructively, we must propose the meanings that are admissible and divide them only into those that are useful to the constructive argument" (ÓRGANON, Topics, L II, III, 110b1, 30-35) [13]. Aristotle had earlier warned that such a constructive argumentative method does not apply to exact rational judgments, for in such cases the purpose of the one arguing matters little. He states that:

> if we are arguing constructively, we must obtain a preliminary admission that if the predicate applies to anything, it will apply universally, provided the claim is plausible, for, it is not enough to argue in a singular case for the purpose of showing that a predicate applies universally (ÓRGANON, Topics, L II, III, 110a1, 35 at 110b1) . [14]

---

[11]DWORKIN, Ronald. *Law's empire*. Cambridge: Harvard University Press, 1986, p. 15.
[12]DWORKIN, Ronald. *Law's empire*. Cambridge: Harvard University Press, 1986. p. 37, 51, 52.
[13]ARISTOTHELES. *Organon*. Translation Edson Bini. 2. ed. Bauru: Edipro, 2010. p. 378.
[14]ARISTOTHELES. *Organon*. Translation Edson Bini. 2. ed. Bauru: Edipro, 2010. p. 377.

Declares that:

> This method is not to be employed always, but only when we are not in a position to state a single argument which applies equally to all cases, as, for example, when the geometrician states that the angles of a triangle are equal to two right angles (ÓRGANON, Topics, L II, III, 110b1, 5). [15]

Thus, to argue or interpret constructively is essential when one intends to build a universal objective according to a purpose that realizes the Justice value, even if other paths are possible, because this is the best way to achieve a human purpose or objective, because the nature of the object requires argumentation with a view to the purpose that one intends to accomplish. Ronald Dworkin, although in the book "The Empire of Law" does not have the purpose of presenting a Theory of Justice, describes how the law acts to accomplish the purposes of a certain community, according to a conception of Justice, highlighting the relevance of several theories of Justice, such as Marxism or utilitarianism, which evidently require principles that are used to fulfill their commitments, being exactly what he recognizes to be the value of these theories [16]

An important part of his study is the relationship between interpretation and law. From there, he begins by presenting arguments about what makes an interpretation of a social practice better than another, and about how a legal exposition promotes a more satisfactory interpretation of this complex and crucial practice[17]. Here, one can already see that without certain principles one cannot interpret the purposes or commitments of a given legal system, revealing the conception of Justice that is inherent to it.

Dworkin presents a conception of Subjective Rights, according to which their enforceability originates from past political decisions, according to

---

[15]ARISTOTHELES. *Organon*. Translation Edson Bini. 2. ed. Bauru: Edipro, 2010. p. 377.
[16]DWORKIN, Ronald. *Law's empire*. Cambridge: Harvard University Press, 1986. p. 76.
[17]DWORKIN, Ronald. *Law's empire*. Cambridge: Harvard University Press, 1986. p. 86.

the best interpretation they may mean to the community, which helps to better explain the complex relationships between law and other social phenomena. Therefore, the content of law depends on the morals and values of the community [18]. Thus, for Dworkin and his Theory of Law as Integrity, the conception of Subjective Rights, in which fundamental rights are included, requires recognizing that these rights belong to people and that they are sponsored by principles that promote the best justification for legal practice as a whole [19], as a corollary, the central role of the Judiciary, within his conception of fundamental rights.

Although Dworkin highlights how the way of exposition of the Judiciary is fundamental to his conception of Law, he does not ignore the role of the legislator in the context of the Theory of Law as Integrity. He first presents two practical moral principles; the first is the principle of Integrity in Legislation, which requires the legislator, when creating norms, to remain consistent with the principles; the second is the principle of Integrity in Judicial Proceedings, which requires judges to analyze and decide norms in a manner consistent with the principles. This principle explains how and why special power should be permitted as proper to courts, explaining why judges should understand the body of law they administer as a whole, rather than as a set of disconnected decisions that they would be free to make or alter one by one [20].

It introduces a third principle, the principle of Political Integrity, provided to guide judicial action according to Law as Integrity. This principle reveals the embodiment of the Community or the State that is directed according to principles of equity, justice and due process of law. It resembles the path of private delivery that people adopt certain convictions, ideals or projects, which may seem a form of metaphysics of poor quality, but taken as a principle, requires

---

[18]DWORKIN, Ronald. *Law's empire*. Cambridge: Harvard University Press, 1986. p. 96.
[19]DWORKIN, Ronald. *Law's empire*. Cambridge: Harvard University Press, 1986. p. 152.
[20]DWORKIN, Ronald. *Law's empire*. Cambridge: Harvard University Press, 1986. p. 167.

recognizing that public officials act on behalf of all members of the community and the need to treat collective responsibility as prior to the responsibility of each of the authorities[21].

Thus, in whichever direction one looks, this theory of Law as Integrity cannot be separated from moral judgments of the community, according to the principles it elects as important. As it recognizes the existence of a community morality, embodied in the legal system, people come to realize that they are not governed only by explicit rules set by political decisions of the past, but by other norms arising from the principles that these decisions assume. An organicity of public norms is created that can expand and contract as needed. This sophistication of the community makes it capable of sensing and exploring what these principles demand in new circumstances, without the need for legislative or jurisprudential change at each point of conflict. Law as Integrity promotes the fusion of political and private circumstances, one as the spirit of the other, promoting the benefit of both [22]

From this exposition, it can be understood that, according to Law as Integrity, legal propositions are true if they stand on or are derived from principles of Justice, equity and due process of law, which promote the best constructive interpretation of the Commonwealth's legal practice, and that such a conception of law only makes sense among people who also desire equity and justice [23].

Thus, it is not possible to sail on smooth seas in constitutional interpretation. The Theory of Law as Integrity not only allows but nurtures various forms of substantive conflicts or tension of the best interpretation of law and when it recognizes that the Integrity of Judicial activity is sovereign over the Law. This is because it desires the recognition of all, as an association of principles, as a

---

[21]DWORKIN, Ronald. *Law's empire*. Cambridge: Harvard University Press, 1986. p. 167, 175.
[22]DWORKIN, Ronald. *Law's empire*. Cambridge: Harvard University Press, 1986. p. 188, 190.
[23]DWORKIN, Ronald. *Law's empire*. Cambridge: Harvard University Press, 1986. p. 225-263.

community governed by a singular and coherent vision of justice, equity and due process of law, in due proportions[24].

It can be concluded that the philosophical attitude of Platonic/Aristotelian thinking manifests itself in Dworkin, when through principles he seeks to fulfill the goal of realization of fundamental rights, revealing the ethical commitments of the community, according to the principles of Justice, equity and due process of law, and meets the goal of realizing the value Justice in a more objective way typical of classical philosophy, by presenting substantial concepts of the ethical values of the community. This is the rational goal that requires principles in the interpretive practice, a common element of Dworkin and the Platonic and Aristotelian theories of Justice, where coherence can only be achieved by the unity of principles that avoid contradiction with the fundamental goals of the community, according to a constructive interpretive practice.

---

[24]DWORKIN, Ronald. *Law's empire*. Cambridge: Harvard University Press, 1986. p. 404.

4. Interpretative Process of Unity Construction and the Figure of Judge Hercules

To deepen the presentation of the role of the Judiciary, in the Theory of Law as Integrity, Dworkin presents the figure of the judge Hercules, who, despite the name of demigod, ceases to be scary when we recognize in him only a method that reflects the special charge of a member of the community, committed to the ethical values of the community embodied in the State, responsible for interpreting the Laws according to the best light, in accordance with the principles that govern the community.

Thus, it is not possible to navigate on calm seas in constitutional interpretation, because founded on principles, the search for unity is one of the most arduous tasks, hence the recourse to the symbolism of the godless, mythological figure of uncommon strength and courage, but even so does not escape feeling the human pain, and to deny in the lament of suffering its discomfiting strength, when by unexpected death is reached, even if moved by revenge against his wife, as expressed by Sophocles, the words of Hercules:

> Go, son, be brave! Have pity on me, worthy of pity for many, that like a girl I bawl in tears - and this no one can claim to have seen me do: I have always followed my woes ingenuously.
> But I, who was such, am now revealed as poor female (Sophocles. The Trachinias) [25]

Now, if the God of uncommon strength reveals his weakness in the face of human pain, despite the many proofs of his uncommon virility, the interpretative task is not safe from imperfection because it is a human task, but

---

[25]SOFOCLES. *The Trachinias*. Translation Flávio Ribeiro de Oliveira. Campinas: Editora Unicamp. 2009. p. 101

one that needs a model of inspiration to guide the challenge of realizing the principles adopted by the community.

It can be concluded, for Dworkin, only through principles one can meet the Herculean challenge of realizing fundamental rights, in which the Courts play a key role of through their interpretation promote its construction according to the best light, revealing the ethical commitments of the community, according to the principles of justice, equity and due process of law.

Plato, in his *Dialogues, does not* present the figure of the Judge Hercules, but also formulates his model of the agent who manages to express the coherence of the whole, guided by reason, which is the figure of Socrates, who is confused with the very destiny of philosophy of placing in the public square the vital problems of the human being.

Although at the end of the Republic after inferring that it is the nature of human beings to pursue the supreme good, of which justice is one of the most outstanding virtues, approaching it to divinity, Plato does not fail to record in Book II, through Glaucus, a certain contractual origin of justice, arising from the need of human beings to regulate their conflicts of interest.

Therefore, the figure Hercules or Socrates serves as a resource to explain that the coherence of the whole is not an easy task, but it is necessary to follow a model that allows achieving coherence and unity for the construction of interpretation, because the laws always arise in order to serve the ideal of justice pursued as a human need[26]however, this is not a solitary task, but a paradigm to inspire the community.

---

[26]"When men reciprocally commit injustice and are victims of injustice, and thus come to experience both, those who cannot avoid the one nor attain the other consider it more advantageous to enter into an agreement so that they will no longer be victims of injustice or come to commit it. From this point, laws and contracts between men are born, and then, what is determined by law is called legality and justice". (PLATO. *The Republic*. 358e-359b) Cfr. *3*. ed. Translation Carlos Alberto Nunes. Belém: Edufpa, 2000. p. 95. (Dialogues). Although in the whole theory of ideas of the Platonic thought the concepts are placed in a more idealized level, justifying his theory of the reminiscence of the ideas that the human soul saw directly in a higher plane, before decaying in this earthly plane, becoming prisoner of the body in a

Recognize the laws as arising from the search of human beings for Justice, which under the argument of Glauco has contractual origin of the rules that govern the conflicts of human beings, does not replace the primary purpose of realizing the principle of Justice. This means that the laws could never be interpreted in themselves, as something detached from the fundamental contract or any other rational foundation, under penalty of transforming the instrument into the purpose, and not take the instrument as a means to achieve the purpose. Therefore, laws can never cease to be interpreted as instruments for the realization of Justice, otherwise they lose their legitimacy.

Within the Platonic *corpus*, the question that there is the possibility of a legitimate government without laws becomes false, because the clear pragmatic function of legislation is the tip of its fragility, being that it should always be in function of a superior end that is only accomplished if human beings are willing to the challenge, whether governors or governed. The fundamental thing is to investigate how the morality of the citizens reflects the organization of the *polis*, because the ethics of the citizens, in classical philosophy, was confused with the ethics before the community.

Remember, prudence is a virtue, so the human being cannot bend as a rational being to a legislation that materializes the unjust, or interpret it in such a way that allows contradicting his nature of being that seeks a supreme end in his existence, because, this way, he would abdicate his rationality. Therefore, Aristotle, despite his empiricist method of observing reality, does not stop, as well as Plato, to observe that there is a finalist character in human

---

world of appearances, when we take the theory of ideas as an epistemological criterion, moving away from understanding it literally as a *real existence of the world of ideas,* it is much easier to understand the richness of the Platonic thought, from which we can extract and interpret the referred passage. For this reason, the Platonic dialogue about knowledge, *Theetetho,* which is apparently inconclusive, clearly points out the various ways in which the human thought can understand and justify the reality that surrounds it in the search for knowledge, in which the diversity of paths has to do with the difficulty that the object of knowledge entails. Cfr. PLATO. *Theetetetus - Tatilus.* Translation Carlos Alberto Nunes, Belém: Edufpa, 2001a. (Dialogues).

activity, as it can be observed since the portico of his work *Nicomachaean Ethics,* in Book I, 1094 a, and 20 [27]

Thus, even in the model of Aristotelian justice defined, usually, as a middle ground between two extremes, taken from Book V [28] of his *Ethics* (Nicomachean Ethics, 1129), justice cannot be interpreted in a simple mathematical character, as simple arithmetic proportion, in which it would be enough to pass a kind of imaginary tape measure between certain conflict situation, and the middle ground found of this clash would be the object to be delivered to the interested parties, realizing the Justice.

In reality, the Aristotelian proportion serves more to demonstrate that Justice can be thought as something rational, as in mathematical operations, although not by the same paradigm, for being a necessity of the human reason.

In fact, even in Aristotelian ethics, the law, as a historical and contingent expression, the reach of the *middle ground* is not enough to configure, through this operation, the achievement of Justice, because already in Book II of the same work, Aristotle is keen to emphasize that in the achievement of virtues, of which justice is the most important, we must necessarily take into account the particularities in *relation to us, that* is, we must take into account the assessment of the fair measure, the middle ground, mainly and fundamentally considering the human being as a historical being.

The middle ground is not a simple measure that in general will be able to meet most human conflicts, it involves equity judgments, as the legislator

---

[27]"It is generally admitted that every art and every investigation, as well as every action and every choice, have some good in view; and therefore it has been very rightly said that the good is that to which all things tend. (...) If, therefore, for the things we do there is an end that we desire for itself and everything else is desired in the interest of that end; *and* if it is true that not every thing we desire with a view to another (because, then, the process would be repeated to infinity, *and* our desire would be useless and vain), *evidently that end will be the good, or rather, the highest good".* (emphasis added) ARISTÒTELES. *Nicomachaean Ethics.* Translation Leonel Vallandro and Gerd Bornheim. São Paulo: Abril Cultural, 1979. p. 49. (Collection The Thinkers, v. 2).

[28]　　ARISTOTELES. *Nicomachaean Ethics.* Translation Leonel Vallandro and Gerd Bornheim. São Paulo: Abril Cultural, 1979. p. 121 (Collection The Thinkers, v. 2).

cannot contemplate all situations in life, being essential the perquisition of the ultimate purpose of human arts, in the case of law, to be an instrument for the realization of Justice. Therefore, the law should always be interpreted in order to achieve Justice[29].

What can result from the *retro* analysis is that the law in antiquity was always perceived as an instrument for the realization of the just. The law was built as a universal element and that served the human purpose of achieving Justice, always subordinated to the end and not the reverse, in which the end as supreme good of Justice had to bend to the contingent (the law) and, therefore, subject to error.

Therefore, it always remained open, because it should be so, the space for the performance of the virtuous human being, who could correct the mistakes of the legislator, attending the end of the legislation to serve as an instrument resulting from the contract or other form of justification of the action among human beings to submit themselves to rules that allow them to live the justice. The realization of justice, before depending on the rules, depends on the action of human beings with sense of Justice, being the rule only a parameter. *And that does*

---

[29]This can be glimpsed in the following passages of the *Nicomachaean Ethics:* "By a middle-ground in the object I understand that which is equidistant from both extremes, and which is one and the same for all men; and by a middle-ground in relation to us, that which is neither too much nor too little - and this is not one and the same for all. For example, if ten is too much and two is too little, six is the middle-ground, considered according to the object, because it exceeds and is exceeded by an equal quantity; this number is intermediate according to an arithmetical proportion. But the middle-ground relative to us is not to be considered thus: if ten pounds is too much for a particular person to eat, and two pounds is too little, it does not follow from this that coach will prescribe six pounds; for that too is, perhaps, too much for the person who is to eat it, or too little - too little for Milo and too much for the beginning athlete. The same is true of running and fighting. Thus a master in any art avoids excess and lack, seeking the middle ground and choosing it - the middle ground not in the object, but relative to **us**" (Aristotle, *Ethics a Nicomachae 1105, 35, 1106.10) (emphasis added).* In Book V, when dealing with equity, Aristotle teaches: "What makes the problem arise is that the equitable is fair, but not the legally fair, but a correction of legal justice. The reason for this is that every law is universal, but about certain things it is not possible to make a universal statement that is correct. In those cases in which it is necessary to speak universally but it is not possible to do so correctly, the law considers the most usual case, although it does not ignore the possibility of error. And not because of this does such a way of proceeding cease to be correct, for the error is not in the law, nor in the legislator, but in the nature of the thing itself, since practical matters are of this kind by nature". (Aristotle, *Nicomachean Ethics, 1137b, 10).* Cf ARISTOTELES. Nicomachaean *Ethics.* Translation Leonel Vallandro and Gerd Bornheim. São Paulo: Abril Cultural, 1979. p. 72, 136. (Collection The Thinkers, v. 2).

not mean free interpretation, but rational performance in the application of the law for the realization of the purpose of achieving Justice.

Justice does not exist if human beings abdicate to act with virtue, not having the habit of performing virtue. It is not by chance that Aristotle builds an ethics of action, practice of virtue. It is not enough to want to be virtuous, you have to practice the virtues. Thus, the achievement of Justice in Aristotle becomes thing of a human practical wisdom, even if guided by the search for the supreme good [30]

There will be no Justice without human beings who do not always and necessarily decide to practice it, applying the laws in order to meet the purpose of the fundamental pact, intending to achieve the *good, freedom, happiness, equality, in* short, the virtue of Justice.

Classical philosophy did not distinguish private ethics from public ethics, although it recognized that there were different spaces of how they were practiced, hence it was fundamental in Aristotelian thought that citizens practiced virtue, considering that political and practical wisdom have the same origin. [31]

Therefore, even if we leave aside the research on whether there is a fundamental convention of human beings that legitimizes the legislative action of the State, as a rational foundation, according to the thought of jusnaturalism, or even if the foundation of the law is the authority according to the rule of

---

[30] "Practical wisdom, on the contrary, is about human things, and things that can be the object of deliberation; for we say that this is above all the work of the man endowed with practical wisdom: to deliberate well. But no one deliberates about invariable things, nor about things that do not have a purpose; a good that can be achieved by action" (*Nicomachaean Ethics*, 1141b, 5-10) Cf. ARISTOTELES. *Nicomachaean Ethics*. Translation Leonel Vallandro and Gerd Bornheim. São Paulo: Abril Cultural, 1979. p. 146. (Collection The Thinkers, v. 2).

[31] "Political and practical wisdom are the same mental disposition, but their essence is not the same. Of the wisdom that concerns the city, the practical wisdom that plays a controlling role is legislative wisdom, while that which relates to the affairs of the city as particulars within its universal is known by the general appellation of 'political wisdom' and is concerned with action and deliberation, for a decree is something to be executed in the form of an individual act" (Aristotle, *Nicomachean Ethics*, 1141b, 25). ARISTOTELES. *Nicomachaean Ethics*. Translation Leonel Vallandro and Gerd Bornheim. São Paulo: Abril Cultural, 1979. p. 147. (Collection The Thinkers, v. 2).

competence, according to positivism[32]we cannot fail to consider that the legal rules are, or should be, made in order to enable the realization of justice, as the supreme good that can be recognized as a principle of the integrity of Law.

The realization of the principle Justice must be built in human action of all possible means, in which is included an interpretive activity that unveils in the laws signifiers that fulfill this purpose, the principle must always be maintained: the law cannot contradict the principle that gave it origin and legitimacy; the law cannot legitimize injustice.

This is the rational goal that requires principles in interpretive practice, a common element of Dworkin and the Platonic and Aristotelian theories of Justice, where coherence can only be achieved by the unity of principles that avoid contradiction with the fundamental goals of the community, according to a constructive interpretive practice.

---

[32] BOBBIO, Norberto. *The Age of Rights*. 19 reimp. Rio de Janeiro: Campus. 1992. p. 21.

5. Rationality and Limits to Judicial Discretion

The figure of Judge Hercules also plays the relevant role of summarizing the function of the Judiciary, because when interpreting the law, Judge Hercules does not seek what he believes to be the best substantive result, but rather the best justification for the past legislative event, according to the best light, recognizing this as an act of a democratically elected legislative power, which must justify the act as a whole and not just the end of the history of the community[33].

Although the Constitution is different from ordinary laws, because it serves as the foundation of other laws, the Hercules Judge, without abandoning his method, must necessarily, in performing his interpretation, proceed to a justification grounded in the deepest elements of the political power of the community, which means that he must seek the best reasons of political theory to support them [34].

Because the issue is faced by such a large scope, the theory of Law as integrity not only allows but nurtures various forms of substantive conflict or tension of the best interpretation of law and when it recognizes that the Integrity of Judicial activity is sovereign over the Law. This is because it desires recognition by all, that there is an association of principles, which enables the community to be governed by a singular and coherent vision of justice, equity and due process of law, in due proportions [35].

What can be seen here is that Dworkin introduces elements that externally condition judicial discretion, since the Judiciary's task is only rational if, when interpreting the principles, it promotes the realization of fundamental

---

[33]DWORKIN, Ronald. *Law's empire*. Cambridge: Harvard University Press, 1986. p. 339.
[34]DWORKIN, Ronald. *Law's empire*. Cambridge: Harvard University Press, 1986. p. 380-404.
[35]DWORKIN, Ronald. *Law's empire*. Cambridge: Harvard University Press, 1986. p. 404

rights, promoting the presentation of substantial concepts of the community's ethical values, which also demands political theory arguments.

When Dworkin presents a series of objections to the conceptions that seek to reassemble the author's thought as the legitimate source of law interpretation. He flatly rejects Originalism. It is not because he is delegating the interpretative task exclusively to judges, and that therefore, there would be a strong discretion of these, on the contrary, it is because he prefers a path where democracy plays a more prominent role, which controls the action of the legislature itself, and logically the Judiciary, whose function is to realize the ethical values of the Community.

The Theory of Law as Integrity is a great abstract model of how one should operate in the interpretation of the rules that characterize the legal phenomena, aiming at a greater good, knowing that these are not dissociated from the morals of the interpreters, who are alive, but making it clear that they are part of a greater project of the community's common history.

A more attentive and open look allows us to glimpse an ambitious project that repositions law among the social sciences as a science that can historically contribute to the construction of the right answer to humanity's great dilemmas.

Therefore, for Dworkin, there is no need for a great return to a memorable moment in history, when great men and citizens threw themselves into these collective goals, and built the Laws, which must necessarily be interpreted as originally posed, this ends up revealing a democratic turning point. It is in this context, that one can understand why the relationship to history is not a nothing, even should serve to build the interpretation of the present, according to principles that are rationally constructed according to the purpose of the interpreter, as a member of the personified community.

This is what allows the construction of an objective element to limit judicial discretion, including the duty of self-restraint of judicial action, despite the recognition of the aspect of creation of law through the Courts, that is, it is part of the process of rationality, to present the criteria by which the judge himself, demonstrates the correctness of the decision.

The issue of controlling judicial discretion is not central in Dworkin, not because he adopts a model of strong judicial discretion, but because it itself is inserted and submitted in the model that governs the creative activity of the Courts, which is only legitimized when it protects the fundamental rights of the community.

In other words, Dworkin resumes the model of classical philosophy that the central issue is not the method, but to explain by means of a model of practical action, what certain substantial contents consist of, what he calls the right answers, and according to these criteria they are legitimized before the *Court of Reason.*

Therefore, it is a serious interpretive error to make the criticism of Dworkin from the element of judicial discretion, because the important issue of its control, is only apparently unavoidable, because it itself is not a central issue, because it follows the form of classical thought, where what matters are the answers that the model allows to produce. This is the focus of theoretical thought.

This type of analysis error, for example, is made by Loiane Prado Verbicaro, who, despite analyzing and comparing very competently several theories on the control of judicial discretion, makes the interpretative mistake of placing Dworkin on the same ruler, failing to observe that Dworkin's question goes through the control of judicial discretion, but only as part of the path to the construction of the integrity of law, or, in other words, reduces Dworkin's question to a methodological question of whether judicial discretion is strong or weak, when in fact Dworkin's thought is a philosophical proposal of how to build the right answer through law, which is different from stating that this is the only right answer, which would deny the historicity aspect of law [36]

This type of criticism ends up being an elaborate means of trying to frame the work under the prism of positivism, which places the central role of law in authority, when Dworkin's theory rightly starts by criticizing positivism, because its scope is to present a form of analysis and construction of law that escapes these theoretical limitations.

According to this ambitious goal, Dworkin needs to present a delimitation of what would be the Creative Power of Courts, associated with other criteria governing law as integrity. As we shall demonstrate.

It is unavoidable at this point to precede with an allusion to Hebert Hart's concept of the open texture of law, according to which there are areas of human conduct in which many things must be left to be developed by courts or officials, who determine the balance in the light of the circumstances, between conflicting interests that vary in weight from case to case, although he points out that such uncertainties may arise with respect to the applicability of any rule to a concrete case. [37]

Apparently, it is the same creative function of the courts by the interpretation process that can be recognized in the cited author, but it is essential to note that it is not the same approach. In fact, Hart explains that the open texture

---

[36]Loaine Verbicaro argues: "The point of conflict refers to the existence, necessity and desirability of judicial discretion in the strong sense, conceived as the possibility of choosing between different courses of action equally valid and admissible, which leads to the absence of a univocal answer" (...) "It is clear that the denial of strong judicial discretion remains empty of meaning. One cannot accept a single decision as correct when one knows it does not exist. It seems more honest to say clearly that the normative standards, more often than not, propose to control it and this, consequently, leads to the election between alternatives that the legal order establishes as interpretative possibilities equally correct and acceptable, as well as to the denial of the thesis of the only answer" Cfr VERBICARO, Loiane Prado. *Judicialization of Politics, Activism and Judicial Discretion.* Rio de Janeiro: Lumen Juris, 2017. pp. 387 and 389

[37]HART, Herbert. L. A. *The Concept of Law.* Translation A. Ribeiro Mendes. Lisbon: Calouste Gulbekian Foundation, 1994. p. 148.

of law is given to judges, even those of the Supreme Court "as parts of a system whose rules are sufficiently determined in the central part to provide standards of correct judicial decision"[38]. That is, it is just a more elaborate garb of obtaining the completeness of the legal system, from the norm in which the interpretation only reveals its content, as determined by the legislature.

Reiterating this distinction, it is worth mentioning that Norberto Bobbio recognizes that the interpretative activity derives from the assumed existence of the legal system as a system, and, for this reason, it is one of the jurist's duties to interpret, in order to not only exclude *incompatible rules,* even if it is impossible to totally exclude antinomies, as well as to promote coherence and completeness of the legal system by the mechanisms of suppression of its gaps[39], however, always and only as the positive law reveals to be insufficient, which presupposes the legal system as a system, it has rules that authorize the judge to fill it, according to the cases analyzed.

The creative function by interpretation, in these cases, is not inherent to the activity of the judge in the act of judging, but an exception provided by law and that thus should be fulfilled faithfully and limitedly, according to the legislative authorization, to complement what is already provided for in the legal system, a concept that is still present in Brazilian law, according to art. 140, caput and sole paragraph, of the CPC, which states that the judge is not exempted from deciding under the allegation of gap or obscurity of the legal system, and that he will only decide by equity in cases provided for by law.

The process of law creation by judges in Dworkin's thought is the one that takes place through the exercise of the interpretive function of law, in the application to concrete cases and that gives life to the content of the law. It not

---

[38] HART, Herbert. L. A. *The Concept of Law.* Translation A. Ribeiro Mendes. Lisbon: Calouste Gulbekian Foundation, 1994. p. 154.
[39] BOBBIO, Norberto. *Theory of the legal order.* Brasília: Ed. UnB, 1995. p. 76,79,80, 117.

only reveals the content of the law, or as it is commonly said the "will of the legislator", but, it recognizes the interpretative performance as essential for the law to assume its true nature, which cannot be denied to judges. Therefore, this activity should be subjected to a rational limit, which is performed through the justification of judicial decisions. It is this duty that deals with the rule of art. 93, item IX, of the CRFB.

It is essential to recognize that for Dworkin, there must be a limit to the process of judicial interpretation, in order to recognize the rationality of the judicial decision in the performance of interpretive activity.

Ronald Dworkin, thus, seeks to limit judicial interpretation, despite recognizing that the interpreter cannot be removed from his preconceptions, from the demonstration of the mechanisms by which the interpreter fulfills ~~the~~ duty to demonstrate that his decision is reasoned, because performed according to the plot of the judicial decisions that precede him, revealing ~~his~~ consistency with the principles of law, demonstrating that the interpretation he presents puts the interpreted object ~~in~~ its best light.

Dworkin holds that fundamental rights will be put in the best light, according to a *constructive interpretation,* which is qualified by having a purpose and which exposes a way of seeing the object interpreted that points in the decision the pursuit of adopting one direction instead of another in order to make it the best possible, a clear case of interaction between the object and the purpose[40].

In accordance with this objective, Dworkin presents the steps to be performed by the magistrate in the decision-making process for a correct interpretation, since Law as integrity rejects the old question whether judges discover or invent the law, but states that they do both at the same time and neither. The judge must identify the rights and duties of citizens created by the community

---

[40]DWORKIN, Ronald. *Law's empire*. Cambridge: Harvard University Press, 1986. p. 52.

embodied according to a conception of justice and equality and must demonstrate that he or she is being consistent with this purpose[41].

The judge does not start from nothing. The community already exists and the act of deciding must mirror its history and desires. Judicial interpretation integrates the continuous history of the chain of law. As the author and critic of this collective work that is the legal system, the magistrate needs to justify his decisions in the principles that govern the embodied community. The first step to fulfill this duty is that his interpretation observes the *dimension of adequacy* by demonstrating how the general set of the community interprets a given legal issue, even though it may detect its incompleteness [42].

The second dimension of interpretation requires that, after the first step, the judge must evaluate and make a judgment on which of these possible interpretative readings allows the work in development to achieve the best possible result, considering all aspects involved[43]. The judiciary's mission in achieving its purpose is thus to justify its choices in the decision-making process by justifying them according to criteria of justice, equity and due legal process, which requires legal principles.

At this point, it can be observed that Ronald Dworkin recognizes in history a prospective meaning, which avoids retrogression in matters of fundamental rights. Dworkin points out that the judiciary has the final word on what the law is, which derives from the function of applying the law to concrete cases, through constructive interpretation. Thus, it plays the most prominent role in a society where there is the rule of law, which is to fix the contours of fundamental rights, according to its best light.

---

[41]DWORKIN, Ronald. *Law's empire*. Cambridge: Harvard University Press, 1986. p. 225
[42]DWORKIN, Ronald. *Law's empire*. Cambridge: Harvard University Press, 1986. p. 230
[43]DWORKIN, Ronald. *Law's empire*. Cambridge: Harvard University Press, 1986. p. 231

Dworkin's description of the elements that legitimize judicial interpretation and its creative role can only be correctly understood from how this creative function of the courts is not isolated from the history of the community, as in Plato's thought, each part of the theory only makes sense if understood as part of a great outline for the construction of the true polis, through recourse to reason whose substantial objective legitimizes the choice of principles that govern the community, according to values elected as important for the welfare of the community.

When Dworkin states that an important part of law is to provide principles for the decisions of the Courts[44], which promote the integrity of the Constitution, it is because the unarmed power is legitimized not for itself, but for the function of contributing to the construction of this project of collective welfare, in a society where the Law reigns.

Thus it is better understandable why the constructive interpretation imposes that choices are made as to why a certain description is better than another or more appropriate for the resolution of the conflict by virtue of the best theory of representative democracy or some other foundation of openly political nature[45], and, according to this line of reasoning, is that it is possible to promote a coherence of ideals of the community, adjusting their interests, without absurd contradictions.

Plato had already pointed out that when thinking with principles it is necessary to seek unity and coherence of thought, despite the movement of the reality that surrounds us, always changeable, because otherwise it is not possible to think the object of reflection in an integral way (Fedro, 249 B-C) [46].

Reflecting this need for coherence when reasoning with principles, Dworkin's Theory of Law as Integrity does not admit laws that adjust the interests

---

[44]DWORKIN, Ronald. *Law's empire*. Cambridge: Harvard University Press, 1986. p. 356.

[45]DWORKIN, Ronald. *A Matter of principle*. 9. ed. Cambridge: Harvard University Press, 2000. p. 163-164.

[46]"Really, the human condition implies the faculty of comprehending what we call idea, that is, to be able to start from the multiplicity of sensations in order to reach unity by means of reflection" cf. PLATON. Greek text John Burnet. Translation Carlos Alberto Nunes. 3. ed. Belém: Edufpa, 2011b. p. 115.

of people in a community according to where they live, the activity they perform, their gender status, date of birth, etc., in which such criteria adopted by the legislature do not follow a reason or principle that gives them internal coherence, revealing contradictions and flagrant dissensions between the various interests in conflict, revealing themselves arbitrary (checkerboard statutes)[47].

When recognizing the interpretative character of law by means of principles, Dworkin resumes, the path that allows the removal of antagonism of principles, and guarantees its exibility and judicial protection, dispensing with the need for intervention by the legislature[48].

The courts should act as Socrates, who, when discussing the most diverse, apparently disconnected topics, such as temperance in the *Carmides,* or friendship in the *Lysis,* at the same time reports the need to proceed with knowledge, and should never depart from such procedure to be guided by ethics[49] . A lapidary phrase of this procedure, Plato describes in the dialogue *Second Alcebiades*, when Socrates enunciates "I was right in saying that the possession of any knowledge unaccompanied by the good can only very rarely be useful, and that most often it harms its possessor" (PLATO, *Second Alcebiades,* 146, X, E) [50]

Precisely because of this, this task of the courts is much more than a presentation of particular answers, but is also a means of moral improvement of the community, because the courts are the rational medium, in which the great moral questions of the community are mirrored and reflected. The community itself can control judicial discretion.

In this broad concept, Law can never be thought of without this connection between substance and procedure, because acting in courts is always

---

[47]DWORKIN, Ronald. *Law's empire*. Cambridge: Harvard University Press, 1986, p. 214
[48]DWORKIN, Ronald. *Justice for hedgehogs*. Cambridge: Belknap of Harvard University, 2011. p. 407.
[49]PLATO. *Carmides - Lysis*. Greek text John Burnet. Translation Carlos Alberto Nunes. 3. ed. Belém: Edufpa, 2015c. (Dialogues).
[50]PLATO. *First Alcebiades - Second Alcebiades*. Greek text John Burnet. Translation Carlos Alberto Nunes. 3. ed. Belém: Edufpa, 2015d. p. 197. (Dialogues).

formal, without having to be formalistic, because the ordinary citizen is not interested in how professionals act before the court, but the professional should be interested in the best way to demonstrate to the court how society mirrors the moral dilemma.

In this sense, there is a fundamental role of Law in creating procedures for the realization of the substantial principles for the realization of the justice value, harmonizing and coordinating this relationship is one of the challenges to be overcome. The approach of a dialectical methodology will lead to the correct understanding of the legal phenomenon, as exposed in Plato's Parmenides dialogue, because the relationship between the multiple and the one, the similar and the dissimilar, movement and rest, birth and destruction, in order to be correctly understood need, first of all, to give little reason for their distinction, but the way the relationship between them occurs, without annulling what is proper to them, contributing to the correctness of thought.

In fact, the dialectical method is thus summarized by Plato:

> In a word, in whatever you suppose to exist or not to exist, or to be determined in any way, you must examine the consequences resulting from this, first, for the object itself, and then with regard to the others: you begin with one, at your own choice, then several, and finally all. The same thing you will do with these others, both in their reciprocal relations and with the object admitted by you each time as existing or non-existent, if you wish to exercise yourself perfectly and thus discern the truth in its fullness (Parmenides, 136, b, c) [51]

---

[51] PLATO. *Parmenides - Philebus*. Translation Carlos Alberto Nunes. Belém: Edufpa, 1974. p. 34. (Dialogues, v. 8). Attentive to this concept of dialectics and uniting it to the Hegelian thought, Gadamer will synthesize that hermeneutics is itself the construction of the happening and the understanding of the thing, for this reason he states: "If our hermeneutic theory seeks to recognize the intertwining of happening and understanding, it will have to go back not only to Hegel, but also to Parmenides". He concludes by describing: *"Thus, the dialectic of question and answer has always preceded the dialectic of interpretation. It is the one that determines the understanding as a happening"* (emphasis in the

This assertion allows stating that before highlighting the distinction between substantive and procedural law, the fundamental to the realization of the value Justice, serving the procedural institutes in their relationship with substantive law, and connected with the moral values and history of the community. It is from this dialectical relationship that you can realize the human welfare by interpreting the conflict posed in front of the Law, achieving Justice.

A constructive interpretation model does not deny and highlights the prominence of the courts in a society in which law reigns. Nor can one believe that law acts beyond the historical situation of men, for law is not like the *receptacle* described by Plato in Timaeus, which:

> receives all things, without ever assuming, in any way, the character of what enters it. By nature, it is the matrix of all things; it is moved and diversified by what enters it, which is why it appears differently according to circumstances (Plato, Timaeus, 50,c)[52].

As it is not the *receptacle, it* is not enough for the Judiciary to declare the right so that, when conflicts come to its analysis and decision, it is enough to change the reality that would suit the best principles of the community, but it is necessary to build mechanisms through which the subjective rights are delivered to the citizens, historically fulfilling the decisions of the community, according to the mechanisms of the judicial process because, if the Judiciary fails in the delivery of the jurisdictional provision for not having adequate mechanisms of execution, its historical legitimacy is not realized[53].

---

original). GADAMER, Hans-Georg. *Truth and Method I*. Translation Flávio Paulo Meurer. 14. ed. Petrópolis: Vozes; Bragança Paulista: Editora Universitária São Francisco, 2014, p. 594, 609.

[52]PLATO. *Timaeus, Critias, The Second Alcebiades, Hypias Minor*. 3. ed. Translation Carlos Alberto Nunes. Belém: Edufpa, 2001b. p. 90 (Diálogos).

[53]The belief that law alone can alter reality was the object of Engels and Kautsky's critique of "legal socialism," cf. ENGELS, Friedrich; KAUTSKY, Karl. *Legal Socialism*. Translation Livia Cotrim and Márcio Bilharino Naves. São Paulo: BoiTempo, 2012.

The very carrying out of the process is a way of controlling judicial discretion, here beyond the aspect of deciding the conflict within the process, since it is always possible that the community may turn against the judicial apparatus, including through the mechanisms of civil disobedience.

6. Distributive Justice and the Promotion of Equality

The system of Public Justice, has a normal pattern of performance, which involves conflicts that Aristotle calls *Corrective Justice*, in which the judge acts as a mediator between individuals, because "corrective justice will be the intermediary between loss and gain", being judges called mediators [54] (Nicomachean Ethics,V,4, 1132a), such standard of decision is applicable, above all, between equals.

But this does not prevent, on the contrary, it makes it necessary that certain situations are supported by models of *Distributive Justice,* which requires principles that aim, precisely, to correct inequalities, according to some principle that is elected as a guide for decision making.

Aristotle himself puts in quotes that this Distributive Justice happens *"according to the merit"* identified by the supporters of a certain political philosophy. Thus, to accomplish Distributive Justice is fundamental the coherence of principles that guide the realization of the solution of conflicts, by promoting equality among human beings that reveal themselves according to the political choices of the community, without implying absolute equality.

In Aristotle's words:

> If they are not equal, they have not received equal things; but this is the origin of disputes and complaints; either when equals have and receive unequal shares, or when unequals receive equal shares. This, moreover, is evident from the fact that distributions must be made "according to merit"; for all admit that the just distribution must agree with merit in some sense, though not all specify the same kind of merit, but the

---

[54]ARISTOTELES. *Nicomachaean Ethics*. Translation Leonel Vallandro and Gerd Bornheim from the English version by W. D. Ross. São Paulo: Abril Cultural, 1979. p. 126 (Collection of the Thinkers, v. 2).

democrats identify it with freemanhood, the partisans of oligarchy with wealth (or nobility of birth), and the partisans of aristocracy with excellence (Ethics., V, 3, 20-30) [55]

When these distinctions of Aristotle's conception of Justice are rescued, it is possible to better understand why Ronald Dworkin is keen to discuss how important the principles of liberalism are for the realization of Law as Integrity, because it is a conception of law that guides concepts of freedom, equality, in a society that does not have high levels of social degradation, and that has high consensus on the political philosophy that conducts its general themes.

However, Dworkin, despite expressly stating that an egalitarian economy is basically a capitalist economy, when expounding the content of *equality,* it is possible for him, without apparent contradiction, when disserting on *freedom,* to state that it is inevitable that some resources belong to the state, and that others must be under public control, to protect them against external factors that corrupt the cost-opportunity ratio. To suggest that certain strict regulations are necessary for pollution control does not imply that he directly supports or denies the advent of a communist society. [56]

Understanding the reasons why Dworkin needs to justify how such principles are realized or should be realized, according to the dominant liberal

---

[55] ARISTOTELES. *Nicomachaean Ethics.* Translation Leonel Vallandro and Gerd Bornheim from the English version by W. D. Ross. São Paulo: Abril Cultural, 1979. p. 125 (The Thinkers Collection, v. 2).
[56] Cf. DWORKIN, Ronald. *Justice for hedgehogs.* Cambridge, Massachusetts: Belknap of Harvard University, 2011, p. 357-375. Still, on the strength of liberalism in Dworkin's thought, see, for example, Chapter 9 of the book Dworkin, Ronald. *A Matter of principle.* Cambridge: Harvard University Press, 2000. p.205-220.A good example of how liberalism has high consensus in the American community is the exposure that Cass Sustein performs to demonstrate how certain paternalistic actions of the State does not hurt the principles that drive this philosophy, even being welcome to promote the welfare of people, according to problems concretely faced by the community, while maintaining the right of free choice of people, what he calls "*soft paternalism*". This does not mean that a society guided by liberalism does not know state intervention, but the interesting of his exposition is to make possible to perceive a conscious search to legitimize these types of interference, to suggest the best choices for the community, aiming at the welfare of all, according to the principles of this philosophical thought, which ends up exceeding the limits of this philosophy, according to a rational argumentation. Cfr. SUSTEIN, Cass. R. Why Nudge? The Politics of Libertarian Paternalism.New Haven: Yale University Press. 2014.

political model of his community, demonstrating the complexity of this philosophy, does not imply accepting that only by this form of philosophical explanation a certain principle becomes valid, on the contrary, when it is possible to demonstrate that by varied conceptions of justice one cannot deny the fundamental importance of a certain principle is because one will be closer to its rational essence, by imposing itself as a necessity for any community to structure itself properly.

It is remembered that even those who try to justify the use of force to legitimize certain political power, cannot ignore the spirit of freedom that dwells in men. Thus, after a brief rescue of how the values of the community influence the political decision process, Nicolau Maquiavel, for example, records that one of the greatest challenges of the Prince who wishes to maintain a conquered kingdom occurs when the:

> become lord of a city accustomed to live in freedom and not to reduce it to ruin will sooner or later be ruined by it: for always harbour in rebellions the name of liberty and its ancient laws, things which are never forgotten, neither for the duration of time, nor for any benefits [57]

In a society with greater tradition, organization and distribution of social goods, with less inequality, even if it goes through historical situations that put the model in check, it may be easier or less difficult to build this relationship with the political principles that are dominant in the community, because it is easier to recognize the political principles of the community as a whole. However, this does not make the result more historically feasible, perhaps it is precisely the opposite that makes the challenge permanent.

---

[57] MAQUIAVEL, Nicolaus. *The Prince*. Translation Mauricio Santana Dias. São Paulo: Penguin Classics; Companhia das Letras, 2010. p. 61.

In this context, pointing out the political choices of the community has a relevant role when one wants to analyze contexts whose responses need a greater scope, according to the Aristotelian distributive justice model, paying attention to this aspect, the means that Dworkin finds to fulfill this goal is precisely by analyzing how certain liberal principles present themselves in his community, although without exhausting its full spectrum.

In a society whose principles of political philosophy that dominate society are better consolidated, it is easier to demonstrate how legal principles embrace with certain principles of a political philosophy, such as: liberalism, Marxism, capitalism etc., but this does not preclude the possibility, that certain subjects may be considered comparatively by these various philosophical thoughts, and build how such principles present themselves as rational in various philosophical conceptions and assert themselves in Law.

There is no conception of political philosophy that can be a priori considered the best, or that dictates the need to consider a given conflict under the gaze of multiple philosophical sources, the point is to show how the unity of argumentation is maintained.

The specificity of the science of Law in contributing to distributive Justice, concretely based, possible to be built, is precisely in that the judicial process is naturally open to the contradictory diversity and debate of political conceptions. Legal argumentation is raised to a singular level of interpretation, which, for this very reason, should be open to hearing and reflecting philosophical conceptions that are not dominant, in order to better construct the right answer.

In this line, when using the Aristotelian philosophy, whose work *The Politics,* for example, despite recognizing slavery as something natural, and by corollary, slaves are placed outside the government, reserved only to free citizens, it is necessary to seek the essence of the argument that is to understand who can conduct politics, which aims to build the happiness of citizens, derived from the degree of equality that free men elect as the most appropriate, because *"society is a meeting of similar beings who have for goal the* most *perfect life possible"*(The Politics, VII, Cap. VII, § 2°, 35) [58].

The goal is not to extract the truth or falsity of Aristotelian arguments, whose interpretation of this major principle allows deducing when the forms of government degenerate denying the achievement of the goal of Politics, but it cannot be denied that Aristotle, according to his method of observation of reality, discusses the organization of the State in order to build the equality possible at his time, exactly the role harvested to the Law, which a historical view allows to critically evaluate the degree of achievement of equality in a given society, exactly what is proposed by Dworkin.

The use of the concept of democratic government, according to Aristotle, is based on the concept of citizen, which nothing more is "the one who can be judge and magistrate" (The Politics, III, Chap. I, § 4°, 20)[59], the place where reigns the equality of access of all to power, because "it would be ridiculous to deny authority exactly to those who have in hands the sovereign power" (The Politics, III, Chap. I, § 5°, 30)[60] , from where democracy is where the concept of citizen is better realized, because destined to eliminate all barrier of access to power and, obviously, of inequality, and that "it clearly results that the citizen is not the same in all the forms of government, and that, therefore, it is in the democracy, mainly, that he adapts to our definition" (The Politics, III, Chap I, § 6°, 1275b, 5) [61]

---

[58] ARISTOTHELES. *The Politics.* Translation Nestor Silveira Chaves. 2. ed. Bauru: Edipro, 2009. p. 243.

[59] ARISTOTHELES. *The Politics.* Translation Nestor Silveira Chaves. 2. ed. Bauru: Edipro, 2009. p. 80.

[60] ARISTOTHELES. *The Politics.* Translation Nestor Silveira Chaves. 2. ed. Bauru: Edipro, 2009. p. 81.

[61] ARISTOTHELES. *The Politics.* Translation Nestor Silveira Chaves. 2. ed. Bauru: Edipro, 2009. p. 81.

The fact that in democracy the sovereign power is in the hands of the poor, according to Aristotle, is a warning that his permanent challenge is to broaden the spectrum of those who can be considered similar, without altering the democratic principle, in which the majority rules, promoting greater equality in the distribution of wealth because, power being in the hands of the majority, if they are equal, democracy is better realized.

The challenge of rethinking democracy today, all the time, is because the poor are still the majority, therefore, permanent source of inequality, but the key is to realize how Aristotelian thought can help the science of law to build principles that solve the problems of inequality, by interpreting the values: equality, freedom and solidarity, according to the current democratic conception, to improve the political society.

Now, if even Aristotle, who recognizes slavery as something natural, does not exclude the servant's dignity as a human being, but only discusses the levels of virtue necessary for each group, stating that "To demand virtue in one and not to demand it in another would be absurd" (*The Politics,* I, Cap. IV, § 10) [62], the more relevant it is for a conception of democracy, in which slavery is unacceptable, the historical construction of equality as an irrenounceable challenge, in which the idea of human dignity is the lever that does not allow the legitimacy of any difference resulting from the capacity of political, economic power, ethnicity, social condition, because human beings are equal in virtue.

This allows Aristotle to recognize the fundamental role of ethics to build the community welfare, and to affirm that "there would be community and some kind of justice even if the State did not exist" (Ethics to Eudemo, Book VII, 10, 25-30) [63], because the respect for human nature is the foundation that legitimates every form of political organization.

---

[62] ARISTOTHELES. *The Politics.* Translation Nestor Silveira Chaves. 2. ed. Bauru: Edipro, 2009. p. 34.
[63] ARISTOTHES. *Ethics to Eudemo.* Translation Edson Bini. São Paulo: Edipro, 2015. p. 280.

It is not to discuss the correctness of the Aristotelian conception in not separating the moral from politics, but to recognize that, when the courts are assigned the role of public instrument of conflict resolution, attracting the use of criteria of distributive justice, it is because, under this aspect, one can no longer detach the decisions of political arguments that require interpretation of the ethical conception of democracy of the political community, because only then can coordinate the various interests that make up society, dragging them to the same end that, according to the Aristotelian conception, would form a virtuous city. [64]

As the function of political rights is to allow discussion of the destiny of the community and not of individuals, from the point of view of contributing to the advancement of democracy, their guarantee is an important and necessary condition for the best defense of fundamental rights, by guaranteeing unequal groups mechanisms of access to power[65].

Ronald Dworkin undertakes this distinction and exercises the development of these arguments of distributive justice, when, for example, removes the contradictions between equality, which even when raised to the level of a sovereign virtue, does not matter the denial or counterpoint limiting the right to freedom, on the contrary, argues as better conception of distributive equality

---

[64]"The city is virtuous, not by chance, but by science and will. However, a republic can only be virtuous when the very citizens who take part in the government are virtuous; now, in our system, all the citizens take part in the government. Thus it is a question of seeing how a man can become virtuous. If it is possible to train in virtue all men at the same time, without taking each citizen apart, this is the best way; because the general drags the particular" (The Politics, Book VII, Chap. XII, § 5°) ARISTOTHES. *The Politics*. Translation Nestor Silveira Chaves. 2. ed. Bauru: Edipro, 2009. p. 253.

[65]That is why Bobbio, when analyzing Hegel's thought, who conceives the State as a higher purpose, highlights the close relationship between the concept of Constitution and the organization of the whole, in which the various parts, even if unequal, make up the people. Cf. BOBBIO, Norberto. *Studies on Hegel*: Law, Civil Society, State. 2. ed. São Paulo: Brasiliense, 1995. p. 99. This view allows us to better understand why, despite these particularities, there can only be effective respect for social and individual rights when political rights are exercised with freedom, where everyone can influence the destiny of the community. Thus, for example, Carlos Ayres Britto points out that, under the mantle of Humanism, a true fusion between collective life and democracy must be sought, raising the civilizing status of the community, promoting the rights of all and especially of the less favored. Cfr. BRITTO, Carlos Ayres. *Humanism as a constitutional category*. Belo Horizonte: Forum, 2007, Chapter IV, p. 31-35.

allows better protection of freedom as an individual right which the citizen can choose the best for their own life, according to a conception of equal consideration and respect for the political community (State) [66]

Resulting from this permanent challenge of the achievement of distributive justice is that even a better structured society needs to be consistent with its fundamental principles in a more rigorous way, and that is what makes it legitimate that Dworkin, from the principle of human dignity, according to the principles of intrinsic value of the human being and personal responsibility, which requires a conscious realization of their own choices, build an acid criticism of democracy in the United States, including proposing reforms of the electoral process and the Supreme Court of the USA, necessary to improve substantially the democracy of its community, beyond the majoritarian criterion [67]

In the same way, Dworkin makes a long exercise of how this principle of human dignity and its unfoldings presents itself as fundamental to properly understand the relationship between ethics and morality underlying several fundamental issues for the welfare of the community, enabling not only a good life, but a good life [68].

This same argumentative line is what allows Dworkin's theory of Law as Integrity, when discussing issues such as euthanasia, abortion, individual freedom, to relate them to other issues, such as affirmative policies, etc., according to certain interpretative principles adopted, by constitutional interpretation, in the grounds of Constitutional Court decisions. Because it recognizes that it is possible that once a principle has been accepted by the legal community, it can and should

---

[66]DWORKIN, Ronald. *Sovereign virtue*: the theory and practice of equality. Cambridge: Harvaard University Press, 2002. especially Chapter 3, The Place of Liberty, pp. 120-183.

[67]DWORKIN, Ronald. *Is Democracy possible here?* principles for a new political debate. Princeton: Princeton University Press, 2008.

[68] DWORKIN, Ronald. *Justice for hedgehogs*. Cambridge: Belknap of Harvard University, 2011.

be applied in cases that are apparently unrelated, even in the most diverse legal fields, according to rational arguments that reveal the unity of the legal system. [69]

Understanding this aspect gives a better view of the contingent of the operation of the Law as an essential element in constructivist interpretation, arising from the natural argumentative limitation in the very historicity of the courts. However, at the same time, this imposes the duty to argue to the limit, so that its contribution to the development of the political community is realised and transparent, even as a source of research for the community in general, subject to a more acid criticism, even by external agents of the legal community, and which should be considered by legal agents, raising the need for its improvement, the objective of legal science.

As seen, one should not believe that all community problems are solved in the courts, but it does not imply escape from the challenge of addressing the broader issues of the community through the analysis of law, and the choice to consciously limit its philosophical speculation, without ignoring that social actors adopt certain principles of political philosophy that influence legislation and other aspects of law.

It is undeniable that the function of law is to reveal the best possible interpretation, through rational reasoning and according to procedural mechanisms, allowing the Judiciary to historically contribute to the realization of Justice, revealing the political and ethical choices of the community[70].

In fact, a conception of Distributive Justice, as exposed, is fundamental for the better understanding of the objectives that are intended to achieve, so that

---

[69]Cf. DWORKIN, Ronald. *Life's dominion*: an argument about abortion, euthanasia, and individual freedom. New York: Vintage Books,1994. Especially chapter 5, p. 118-146.

[70]As already stated Dallari "In fact the law is always political, for its origins and its effects on individuals as necessary participants of coexistence, with their values and their interests that are only realized in the social, as well as on social groups and society as a whole". Cf. DALLARI, Dalmo de Abreu. *The Power of Judges*. 3. ed. São Paulo: Saraiva, 2008, p. 59.

the Judiciary is adequate to the new demands of post-industrial society, presenting itself as the rapid and competent guardian in the tutelage of community interests.

When it does so, the court expresses political choices already made by the community, generating gains for the citizenry, by allowing them to decide on the Rights they possess, without affecting the fields of political decision-making made by the Legislative and Executive branches, and according to a consistent political argument sustained on the basis of this principle [71]

---

[71]DWORKIN, Ronald. *A Matter of principle*. 9. ed. Cambridge: Harvard University Press, 2000. p 27, 57.

7. Conclusion

The task of finding connections between the work of Plato, Aristotle and Dworkin, allows us to observe how originality is often in resuming classical paths that still influence Western thought, following the great lines in finding the supreme good, or the right answer, so that human beings can fully live their humanity, object since always of philosophy.

Only by following this path is it possible to reposition the role of Law in the set of human sciences, claiming a noble object, which is the rational construction of legal principles as a mirror of the community's ethical choices.

To obtain this result, the approaches on fundamental rights must follow the following script of analysis, scrutinized retro, as a result of a philosophical-legal journey towards the full realization of human rights:

1- *Overcoming the Madness of TOT* - It is necessary to overcome the *curse of Tot of* the interpretation of fundamental rights, building its substantial content beyond the reading of the constitutional text, highlighting the role of the interpreter to reveal the written text, which without it says nothing, which is mute and no other way can find to express the purposes and values of the community, recognizing the Law as the most competent interpretive practice to bring objectivity to the ethical choices of humanity.

2- Philosophical Attitude and Constructive Interpretation - it is necessary to adopt a philosophical attitude towards normative conflicts, identifying the legal principles that allow finding the truth, in the formulation of the right answer, ruling out all forms of skepticism, arguing in a constructive way to find the substance of fundamental rights, even if not expressly stated in the constitutional text, allowing citizens to judicially seek their protection, as authentic subjective rights.

3. Interpretative Process of Unity Construction - The method of interpretative analysis should always be committed to the ethical values of the community embodied in the State, and as such in the interpretation of the Laws, because it is founded on principles, it should be guided in the search for unity, however difficult the task may be, in view of human imperfection, according to a model of inspiration to guide the challenge of realizing the principles adopted by the community, as a resource to make explicit the coherence of the whole, according to the ideal of justice of the community.

5. Rationality and Limits to Judicial Discretion. - The emphasis on the function of the Judiciary, which is responsible for the last word in the interpretation of the law, arising from its law-creating activity, requires indicating the rational criteria that limit judicial discretion. It is these elements that allow the control of judicial discretion and that is legitimized when it protects the fundamental rights of the community, which can be investigated according to rational criteria. They are the following dimensions to be observed:

5.1.The *dimension of adequacy* demonstrating how the general set of the community interprets a given legal subject, even though it may detect its incompleteness. To this end, it should observe in its interpretation, among others:

a) How the past legislative event is considered, recognizing this as the act of a democratically elected legislature, and that it should be analyzed as a whole and not just as the end of the community's history.

(b) as the Constitution, though different from ordinary laws, because it serves as the foundation of other laws, has its interpretation justified from the deepest elements of the political power of the community, according to the best reasons of political theory.

5.2 The *dimension of Rationale* that requires, after the first step, the judge to evaluate and make a judgment about which of these possible interpretative readings allows the work in development to achieve the best possible result, considering all aspects involved. In his interpretation, he should demonstrate:

a) That the decision addressed all the substantive arguments of the conflicts, producing a coherent vision of justice, equity and due process of law, in due proportions, so that the protection of fundamental rights, results in substantial concepts of the ethical values of the community.

b) The decision is presented in such a way that the community can not only observe the procedure, but can capture in the decision the common history of the community, which is not a nothing.

5.3 In this regard, moreover, the need for consistency prevents the judge from admitting laws that adjust the interests of persons in a community according to the place where they live, the activity they carry out, their gender status, date of birth etc., since such criteria adopted by the legislator do not follow a reason or principle that gives them internal consistency, revealing flagrant contradictions and dissensions between the various interests in conflict, and proving to be arbitrary.

Distributive Justice and the Promotion of Equality. - The full realization of fundamental rights goes beyond the normal pattern of judicial action, in which the judge acts as a mediator between equal individuals. It also requires the performance by the model of *Distributive Justice,* which requires principles that aim to correct inequalities, according to the principle that is chosen as a guideline for decision making.

6.1 Distributive Justice, is realized by the coherence of principles that guide the realization of the solution of conflicts, aiming at the promotion of equality between human beings according to the political choices of the community, without implying absolute equality, and requires a reflection on the dominant political model in the community, but without closing itself to the analysis of other minority thoughts, demonstrating how the legal principles embrace with certain principles of political philosophy.

6.2 A model for the protection of fundamental rights must always include the principle of democratic government, based on the concept of citizenship, where equal access to power for all prevails, an expression of popular sovereign power, aimed at eliminating any barrier to access to power and, to eliminate inequalities.

6.3 The construction of the political rights, allow to discuss the destiny of the community and not of the individuals, but without importing, contradictions with the individual rights, where the best conception of distributive equality allows the best protection of the individual right which the citizen can choose the best for the own life, according to a conception of equal consideration and respect by the political community (State).

These practical moral principles of the constructive interpretation model allow the science of law to be elevated to a differentiated level among the social sciences, as it is the science responsible for giving objectivity to the moral choices of the embodied community.

From this, the teaching of Law itself should be impacted to have as object to analyze the great ethical issues faced by the Courts, material and procedural Law are only tools of interpretation, whose interfaces reveal the ethical choices of the historical society, on the way to achieve the right answer, thus, Law is an archeology of the present of the ethical choices of the past, reflected in the present and prospective of the future.

In defining the promotion of fundamental rights as the objective of legal science, this is in keeping with the direction indicated in the Brazilian case since the constitutional preamble, whose desideratum is to build a *Democratic State, destined to ensure the exercise of social and individual rights, freedom, security, well-being, development, equality and justice, as supreme values of a fraternal, pluralistic and unprejudiced society, founded on social harmony and committed, in the internal and international order, to the peaceful resolution of conflicts.*

And in this step, a systematic interpretation of laws requires referring to the constitutional principles of the Federative Republic of Brazil, both because it is the fundamental legal-political document of the country, but, above all, because only through its interpretation allows the Democratic State of Law to advance in its foundations, notably citizenship, human dignity, social values of work (art. 1 of CRFB).

This allows theoretical breath for an analysis that goes beyond a national legal system, fundamental for the interpretation of International Human Rights Treaties and their relationship with national systems, essential for the correct interpretation of Brazilian law, whose positive law does not establish a relationship of conditionality between the fundamental rights, in addition to stating that they have immediate application, whose rights expressly provided for do not exclude others arising from the regime and the principles it adopts, or from international treaties to which the Federative Republic of Brazil is a party, as provided in §§ 1 and 2 of art. 5 of the CRFB.

In this diapason, it is considered that the deep inequality that still prevails in Brazilian society and that would shame even the most convinced liberal of the eighteenth century facilitates the waiver of greater theoretical scope to justify certain historical achievements that will be affirming beyond the model of political philosophy adopted, eventually, by the interpreter, whose role in law is to reflect the interpretive process of the historical achievement of justice, as a rational requirement, based on arguments of political philosophy, debated and demonstrated by various biases its rationality.

In fact, it is relevant to state that, according to the Brazilian tradition, one cannot deny the function of the courts in saying the law, therefore, defining the contour of fundamental rights without affecting the function of the Executive and Legislative Powers, even because these Powers are independent and harmonious, as postulated in art. 2 of the CRFB.

Recognize this constructive interpretive function of the Judiciary is particularly important in a country whose history is marked by institutional discontinuities and long periods of dictatorship, which taught that the safeguard of fundamental rights can only have effective defense with a judiciary that can, freely, exercise this mistery, and when, in this field, fails the rationality, definitely is a reflection of serious failure in building the community embodied for the realization of the value Justice.

The current concept of democracy puts humanity on the path to be governed by a philosophical thinking, in which unarmed Power expresses rational ethical choices, so that those who do not have access to other forms of Power have security that this is of equal access to all, which makes relevant the strengthening of the role of the International Courts of Justice, in permanent dialogue with the Local Courts, demonstrating that force is never a good source of answers, but Justice, so that society has chosen to live under the rule of Law.

8. Bibliographical references

ARISTOTELES. *Metaphysics*. Translation Vinzenzo Cocco and notes by Joaquim de Carvalho. São Paulo: Abril Cutural, 1979. Book II.(Collection the Thinkers).

__________. *About the soul*. Translation Ana Maria Lóio. São Paulo: Martins Fontes, 2013.

__________. *Organon*. Translation Edson Bini. 2. ed. Bauru: Edipro, 2010.

__________. *Nicomachaean Ethics*. Translation Leonel Vallandro and Gerd Bornheim. São Paulo: Abril Cultural, 1979. (Collection The Thinkers, v. 2).

__________. *A Política*. Translation Nestor Silveira Chaves. 2. ed. Bauru: Edipro, 2009.

__________. *Ethics to Eudemo*. Translation Edson Bini. São Paulo: Edipro, 2015.

ATIENZA, Manuel. *El sentido del derecho*. Barcelona: Ariel, 2004.

BOBBIO, Norberto. *The Age of Rights*. 19 reimp. Rio de Janeiro: Campus. 1992.

__________. *Teoria do ordenamento jurídico*. Brasília: Ed. UnB, 1995.

__________. *Studies on Hegel*: Law, civil society, state. 2. ed.

BRITTO, Carlos Ayres. *O Humanismo como categoria constitucional*. Belo Horizonte: Forum, 2007.

DWORKIN, Ronald. *The Empire of Law*. São Paulo: Martins Fontes, 1999.
__________. *Law's empire*. Cambridge: Harvard University Press, 1986.

__________. *A Matter of principle*. 9. ed. Cambridge: Harvard University Press, 2000.

__________. *Justice for hedgehogs*. Cambridge: Belknap of Harvard University, 2011.

__________. *Sovereign virtue: the theory and practice of equality*. Cambridge: Harvaard University Press, 2002.

__________. *Is Democracy possible here?* principles for a new political debate.

Princeton: Princeton University Press, 2008.

__________. *Life's dominion: an argument about abortion, euthanasia, and individual freedom*. New York: Vintage Books,1994.

ENGELS, Friedrich; KAUTSKY, Karl. *O Socialismo jurídico*. Translation Livia Cotrim and Márcio Bilharino Naves. São Paulo: BoiTempo, 2012.

GADAMER, Hans-Georg. The *idea of good between Plato and Aristotle*. Translation Tito Lívio Cruz Romano. São Paulo: Martins Fontes, 2009.

__________. *Truth and Method I*. Translation Flávio Paulo Meurer. 14. ed. Petrópolis: Vozes; Bragança Paulista: Editora Universitária São Francisco, 2014.

HART, Herbert. L. A. *The Concept of Law*. Translation A. Ribeiro Mendes. Lisbon: Calouste Gulbekian Foundation, 1994.

MAQUIAVEL, Nicolaus. *The Prince*. Translation Mauricio Santana Dias. São Paulo: Penguin Classics; Companhia das Letras, 2010.

NUNES, Benedito. *The overcoming of Philosophy* In O Dorso do Tigre. São Paulo: Ed 34, 2009.

PLATO. *Fedro*. Greek text John Burnet. Translation Carlos Alberto Nunes. 3. ed. Belém: Edufpa, 2011b.

__________A *Republic*. *3*. ed. Translation Carlos Alberto Nunes. Belém: Edufpa, 2000. (Dialogues)

__________. *Theetetho - Cratil*. 3. ed. Translation Carlos Alberto Nunes, Belém: Edufpa, 2001a. (Dialogues).

__________ *Carmides - Lysis*. Greek text John Burnet. Translation Carlos Alberto Nunes. 3. ed. Belém: Edufpa, 2015c. (Dialogues).

__________ *First Alcebiades - Second Alcebiades*. Greek text John Burnet. Translation Carlos Alberto Nunes. 3. ed. Belém: Edufpa, 2015d. (Dialogues).

__________. *Parmenides - Philebus*. Translation Carlos Alberto Nunes. Belém: Edufpa, 1974. (Dialogues, v. 8).

__________. *Timaeus, Critias, The Second Alcebiades, Hypias Minor*. 3. ed. Translation Carlos Alberto Nunes. Belém: Edufpa, 2001b. (Dialogues).

SOFOCLES. *The Trachinias*. Translation Flávio Ribeiro de Oliveira. Campinas: Unicamp Publisher. 2009.

SUSTEIN, Cass. R. Why Nudge? The Politics of Libertarian Paternalism.New Haven: Yale University Press. 2014.

VERBICARO, Loiane Prado. *Judicialization of Politics, Activism and Judicial Discretion*. Rio de Janeiro: Lumen Juris, 2017.

Printed by Books on Demand GmbH, Norderstedt / Germany